What Is a Whale?

Written by Michèle Dufresne

PIONEER VALLEY EDUCATIONAL PRESS, INC.

What is a **whale**?

Is it a fish?

No! Whales are **mammals**

just like us!

Like all mammals, whales use lungs to breathe. They also give birth to live babies.

3

Look at the whale.
The whale hits the **water**
with its fin.
Whack! Whack! Whack!

When the fin whips
the water, it goes
swish, swish, swish!

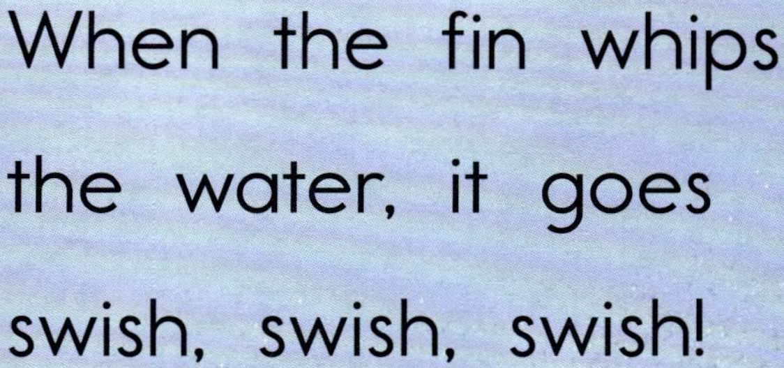

A whale will
sometimes hit the
water's surface
with its tail or fin.
It may be warding
off predators.

With a flick and a whisk, the whale flips the **seal** into the water!

When hunting seals, whales sometimes use their flippers to push a seal into the water.

Look at this big whale.
It is going to gulp up some krill,
which are small **animals**.

Baleen whales have no teeth. They have plates of baleen instead. These whales take in large mouthfuls of water full of krill, then push the water out the sides of their mouths. The baleen traps the krill so the whales can eat it.

How many whales are there?

Look at this graph.

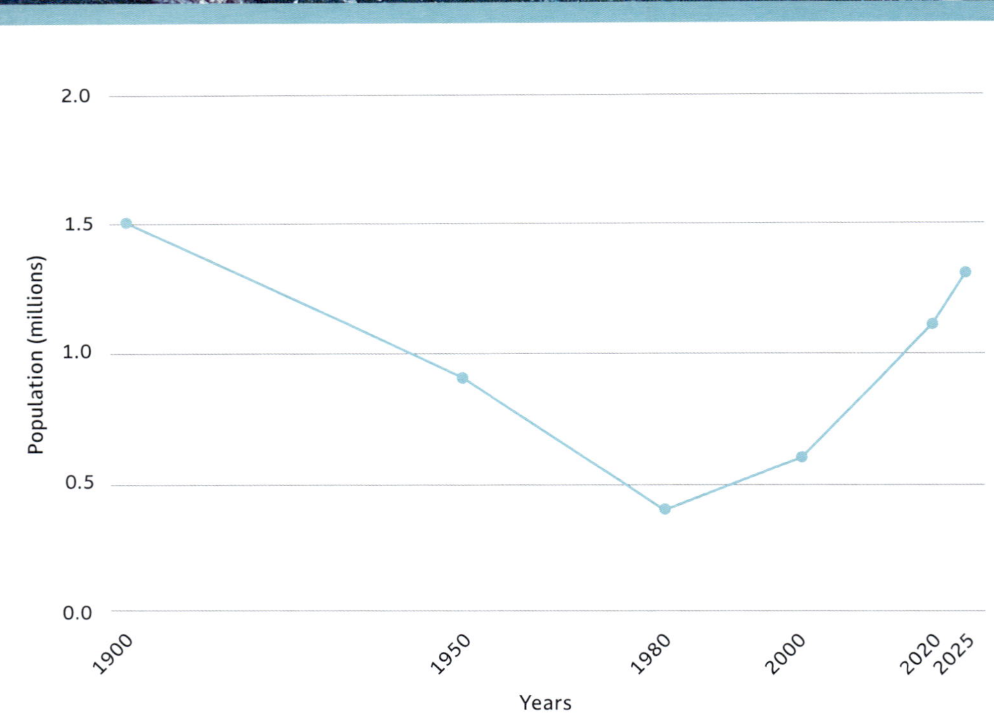

The water is full of whales!

For many years, the number of whales declined. Now thanks to new laws, whales are protected, and their numbers are growing again.

glossary

whale

mammals

water

seal

animals